# Keeping Time

*Poems by Judith Moffett*

**Louisiana State University Press**
*Baton Rouge    1976*

*10/1978*
*cpt. alex.*

Designer: Dwight Agner
Type face: VIP Trump Mediaeval
Typesetter: Graphic Composition, Inc., Athens, Georgia
Printer and binder: Moran Industries, Baton Rouge, Louisiana

"Requiem for Any Possible Thing" originally appeared in *Contemporaries* (Viking, 1972).

"Cows and Corn," "Wash in Eight Colors," "Glossolalia," "Indecent Exposure," "Comeupance," "Cecropia Terzine," "Plaint of the Summer Vampires," "Diehard," "Signatories," and "Bending the Twig" originally appeared in *Poetry*.

"Lake Poem" originally appeared in the *New Yorker*.

Other poems in this volume originally appeared in *Bits, Carolina Quarterly, Contempora, Georgia Review, Hollins Critic, Iowa Review, Journal of General Education, Mill Mountain Review, Minnesota Review, Parenthése, Pebble, Shaman, Southern Poetry Review,* and *Wind.*

PS
3563
O29
K4

LIBRARY OF CONGRESS CATALOGING IN PUBLICATION DATA

Moffett, Judith, 1942–
    Keeping time.

    I. Title.
PS3563.029K4      811'.5'4      76–28256
ISBN 0–8071–0198–2
ISBN 0–8071–0254–7 pbk.

*for Ed, Catherine, and Jimmy*

## TELLTALE

Precarious as Moroni on his spire,
Lacking the gold-leaf hide, the golden horn,
And the sweet certainty of being upborne
By an angelic nature or a stout wire

Harness come earthquake, chaos, gales that blow
Fiercest up where the wingless angel stands,
Above you, mortal trinity of friends,
I play my trump and pivot on one toe.

That I may crown and bless the teepee-form
Chapel your three lives, touching at their tips,
Brace under me embracing mine, the lips
Which shaped warm words and kissed me, never warm

Until you Father, Mother, Alien,
None blood-kin, kindled fires in that blood,
Now founded in the bracing wind on God
(Since God is love), and like a weathervane

Whose trust is telling how the winds blow truly
Not what it wishes: take these words for what
They're worth. If love's a sign of holy writ
The windiest words I wrote of you were holy.

# Contents

## III

I

## Glossolalia

(30 August 1972)

I    No spirit drove me to this wilderness.
Not starved or tempted here, I ramble, write,
Brew tea and tend the blazing in the grate
And think about my life, made meaningless

By faith's demise. Fire fretting cozily,
Teacup abrim, I'm warm, content, alone.
It's morning. Down the mountainside, sunshine
Inches toward my shadowed roof; and I

Am thirty, it's my birthday—of them all
Since Jesus the most difficult. Today
A firm voice, mine, calls time and puts away
Its stopwatch: time it means for parable,

For miracle, time to embrace a mission
Prepared-for thirty years. Somehow I can't
Gainsay the godalmighty precedent
That pressed on me this craving for vocation.

II   Born to a secular and prosaic age
We'll never watch a camel-skinned wild man
Come striding from his wilderness at noon
To officiate at the lovely *rite de passage*
Named in his name. No barefoot honey-fed
Wild John; no luminous dove to spiral down,
Down, through the great voice booming *Yes: this one
Is mine all right* and then *So far so good*

And brush a perfect wing across our eyes;
No sign, in fact, at all: such poetry
Has vanished from the world. Instead tonight
Thirty sharp, tiny tongues of fire will rise
To eloquence at once, wag frantically,
And, when I breathe the wish, at once wax mute.

III   What joy, what comfort! In the grate
Soft bickerings and forking light;
Fierce heat throbs from the fireplace-stone;
For joy the kettle clears its throat
And flips its lid! These moments when
Life seems so rich and splendid on
Quite mortal terms, how odious
To draw divine comparison!

True. Yet it draws itself; alas
Lord Christ that thou art merciless!
The spattering sparks shoot up and die,
The voice cries in the wilderness
No more, not ever. Should it cry
The whole wrenched cosmos, violently
Charged meaningful, would thrum with joy
And so would I, and so would I.

At first blush, discomfiting
To turn so beyond belief
Credulous no time after the creed
Failed than which anything

Must have seemed less
Unbelievable—Yeti, UFO
Spacecraft, witchcraft,
Monster in Loch Ness—

Till time told why
Any world's more likely
Than one whose truths all
Always meet the eye.

I   Suppose for argument's sake that we
survive. As *us*. Neither pure energy restored
to the bosom of the Life Principle, nor cemetery
crabgrass, nor half a century's
labor among the lepers—but
us: ourselves. And suppose then
how we'd eternally get on without books,
without style or beautiful things or
work that needs doing, Brahms, weather,
the turns of seasons; never again
to sight three elk sighting you
from the high end of a high meadow's
steep slope, Indian paintbrush burning in grass
lush and high as hay. . . . Afterlife's
got to be life in the Hereafter,
life-after-death, life "beyond the grave"
and the thing a grave keeps; how can afterlife not be
losing substance and sensation, and so losing
touch, contact, with everything that makes life
of a richness desirable for ever and ever,
world without end? Fearful gift, thankless favor:
to be spared oblivion, having lost the world,
merely to shuttle between grief and deadly
boredom, sounding loss to the bottom
from everlasting to everlasting.

Et in Arcadia ego? Yet so very
often dwelling in a house of
flesh turns out not
to be one bit arcadian. Death's
as much the end of
multiple sclerosis as it's
the end of multiple
orgasms, and if we should
somehow survive our
dereliction, well, I
for one can think of things less
tedious than being
eternally rid of colostomy
bags, cattle prods, and metal
hands.

II     *Quinci si può veder come si fonda*
*l'esser beato ne l'atto che vede,*
*non in quel ch'ama, che poscia seconda . . .*
    *Paradiso,* XXVIII, ll. 109–111.

    . . . for God is love.
    I John 4:8

Good Christian poets and seers have versified
Their certainty of a life "beyond the grave"
For centuries. It felt heavenly to write
One's most immortal lines about having died.

Few poets had more to say than Milton had,
Who (young, still sighted) in "Lycidas" concludes
The word is love   *Blake's word*   though people thought
Milton a genius, and that Blake was mad.

Judged by his versicles and boneless nudes
Blake *was* a wierd impractical crackpot.
*The bow of burning gold   The pebble and clod*

Milton knew politics. Universal Love
In England? Rubbish. Dante started with light
Like John the Revelator, but stopped with God.

John, upon Patmos, glimpsed by second sight
The foursquare city of gold like yellow glass
Whose gates were pearls, whose jasper ramparts stood
On twelve studded foundations: chalcedony, chrysolyte,
Amethyst, emerald   *A Hell in Heaven's despite*
*If ever one was built*   —but John was a poor man.
He did write also, in wretched Exile's Greek,
"The Lamb was the light thereof. And there shall be no night."

Blake's New Jerusalem meant love, and Blake
Knew poverty and angels as well as John,
But denied the punishing fire. *So which view's right?*
To see to love enlightenment: their synthesis.
*Then Heaven would be—?* Where God is, Hell where God
Is not. *And God is—?* Love. *And light?* And light.

Source of all warmth and light, Intelligent Love,
One Geminus that feels and one that thinks
Joined at the heart and brain; of equal worth
Though Castor's noun and Pollux adjective.

And we perpetually present to them, alive
Like gilled carp pumping the compound aqueous element
We'll change into ourselves; let *self* still be
In Heaven! *The Lamb's the light thereof*

*Is Love*   Call Heaven where love is ambient,
Where incorporeal lovers perfectly
May meld some way the fumbling hand-in-glove
Of sexual union gropes toward blindly on earth,
Forging as best it can its tingling links
*You'd lose those*   Something luckier would survive.

*WILL it be luckier?*
                         "Would," not "will." I've planned
This heavenly blueprint of what matters viewed
Sub specie aeternitatis, searched
The texts and pretexts, so's to understand
What matters *now*. John's gold-glass Disneyland
Shines with its useful truth, however crude
The metaphor, for the disabused de-churched
Mortal, slave to a red sweep-second hand.

Stevens averred we uninsurables "die
For good," and I agree
Given that "good" means "ever"; and would begin
*Now* to love love and light, and life, as I
Anticipate no vitam venturi saeculi
To love them in.

> The heart is deceitful above all things, and
> desperately wicked: who can know it?
> Jeremiah 17:9

*Luce intellettual, piena d'amore*
Sings Dante (or sings Beatrice) in Glory.

Switch *luce* and *amore* round instead:
Love full of light, heart set ahead of head.

Quibbling, you'd think? Duns Scotus and St. Thomas
Thought it a crucial quibble—check the *Summa*'s.

Cherish them both! How many souls respect
Emotion but disparage intellect.

—As though the jealous rage, the victim's shrieking,
The torturer's glee, weren't heartfelt, rightly speaking.

Deceitful, wicked heart, the Psalmist knew,
Who loved Bathsheba, what you tempt us to.

Be noun, come first, but full to spilling over
With "intellectual light." Sweet Reason's lover.

## Carol
### (Erie, Pennsylvania)

Snow-shrouded town of Erie
Thy lake lies blue as steel,
While over us ubiquitous
The broken snowclouds wheel;
Yet through its dark thoughts, ghostlike,
The sails of summer skim
And grieve their lake, by slow mistake
Gone brittle at the brim.

Too like this wintry city
We dwell heart-deep in snow;
Grow lovesick for the sun; endure
Our lake's dumb grief also.
We must go undefended,
We have to stay thawed through:
What hopes and fears of all the years
Can meet, unless we do?

# In Therapy
*for J. A., Ph.D.*

Fur upon chin and lip, wig talcumed, one
Gold earring dangling, who is this beneath
Whose punctured skin an ink-green girlie bumps
Upon a bicep? Every child of man
Decks him in man's own image: breasts and rumps
Swaddle him as a winding sheet its wraith;
Unwrap that specter like a tangerine
And whose child might have eyes to see it with?

His gilt-framed mirrors reproduce
Most faithfully the stiffly sprouting hair,
Preoccupations, quirks, tics, prickly heat,
Pockmarks and clammy palms of my disease,
And certainly agree I am not fair
Though of the walking wounded. Hungry fleas
Of panic surf along my spine in sweat
Whenever my eyes skid off his face.

And he is ineluctable. The feet
So lately flexed for spiraling berserk
Inside the hollow needle of the dark
With a fly's desperate cunning, start by degrees to bring
Their gaunt starved beast toward where the opaque
Witch-doctor, silver-corseted to the throat,
Flings kindling on a distal eye of light
Then stiffly crouches by it, glittering.

Two eyes, a staple-wound on a black hide,
Watch the mosquitoes die for love of it—
The red-and-yellow wincing in the bright
Barrera—and are held at bay. Outside
The charméd circle howls their beast: Undo!
Burst like a cloud in splinters, needle-white
As rain, as rising salmon, so I may, freed
From all I turn you into, turn to you!

So when at last
Those slick sharp sails have slit the black
Behind my eyes and set their corners in
And I have borne enough with each again

They lift, fill stiffly, glimmer past
From dark to darkness, lid to shut
Lid. Dozens of places where my mind is cut
Begin to close, begin to cut them back.

## Scanning the Lines

*for Edward Lueders*

I   Time, uncompromising realist,
refines the noncommittal blur
of flesh we are from birth, seeking the buried bone.
Inside our skin somewhere
a face is trapped, the one most truly ours,
the bust
sealed in the clay cocoon,
which underneath Time's fingers, deft and merciless,
in time emerges winged. Whatever glowers
at last or shines through the slashed flesh is us,
our very selves; our sculptured faces grow
increasingly translucent, luminous, true,
modeled from inside out, from outside in.

And beauty lying no deeper than the skin—
mere mask of youth—collapses, melts like candlewax,
tried out by Time. Time will have nothing less
than truth: whose beauty breaks
in pieces like an icefloe late in spring,
gouged nose to chin by Time's incisive nail,
was never beautiful.
Beliefs, deeds, artifacts, loves, everything
held dear must be Time-tested. Time will tell
their worth, and ours as well;
in time
we'll look like who we are, be who we seem,
wrought down to soul and skull.

2    I think of the beautiful old people I know:
fierce, deliberate, wry,
tree-tall Catherine; Harlan with the blunt nose
for mannerly nonsense; Anna, snowy and rose,
whose friends do nothing disagreeable. I think of you
and how in twenty years you will be old.
The wedding slides and yearbooks hold / withhold
a bland, attractive youth
who might—how could one tell?—be or become
con man, attorney, crook, bank president, bum.
And now your children wear that smooth
ambiguous look, while year by year you grow
more wholly, surely, truly beautiful.

Beauty invests the grooves carved parallel
and fanwise in your face,
channels beauty will deepen, riverlike,
dazzling the eye of the beholder—not
deceived for once by what,
except through sorcery, age cannot fake—
till you are one of the beautiful old men.
A good ten years I've watched the light increase,
the creases ramify, the hair burn white
above a harmony of bone and skin
suffused with kindness breaking, brightening, stinging
swift rise of tears, perpetually springing
free of the chrysalis in pouring light.

By two a.m. the haggled birds
And tart smirch of brightness deeply bowled
Had blurred. A murky bottle, cigarettes, sisal words
Braided a lanyard, gray and gold,
In four, in three, gradually twisting round
Into one smoky fibrous strand . . .

Hours earlier I, an usher, had prised away
And borne into the kitchen on a tray
The sherry glasses of the communing host;
Our hostess sliced a brace of turkeys crisped.
Now usher-sober, slack (being overdosed
By half a bitter pill) I knew my shoulder possessed

Without ado. Her deep tired voice rasped
Mm.   Mm.   into the rope of smoke.
Crisp hair, silver and slate,
Poised a usual profile. Shaken to the root
I felt, bent sinister beneath it, the hand stir, stroke
Dumb and instinctive as a swan or cat.

*Ribs, hunching tendons enclose*
*A famine worrying its dish of scraps*
*Seasoned with* Meproban *ground fine, the dose*
*Only just tolerable, discreetly. The laps*
*It longs to climb into, is too long for!*
The trick, of course, is this: to seem no more

Astute than anything crimped to cygnet's shape
About the shining wings and sinuous nape
Whose grace it lives by—any hank of new fur
Drownable, blind, tongue-buffeted to breath
About the rhythm and tongue
And its own skittering heartbeat; even to swap
Gratefully, with joy, the luxury of truth
For this mute, incidental cherishing.

When finally I'm up she's there still: fifty-five
gray and stout, lingering over cool coffee
and the morning paper. She
is six children's mother, and though I love
her as if she were mine,
she's not. I might go kiss her now, I realize; again

the bald thought terrifies. My stomach, recoiling,
kinks and cramps, both palms sweat
themselves cold. At the stove I put
an egg in a pan of water. She glances up, tells me good morning,
sips from her cup. Should I try it now?
An arm around her, smack on the cheekbone? No,

her hand rubs her face, she starts a conversation.
Absurd, I scold my viscera irritably,
why should she mind, mightn't it please her? *Crap!* they say
*don't give us that. This situation
is, for you, exactly as world-shaking as you guess.*
More charged with purpose I pour a glass

of milk and take it to the table. Now?
No, for now she has risen, goes to dress,
and now the idea of *kiss*
can brace itself to endure the next chance. Whew.
Reprieved, I slump in a chair,
chew and unclench all over after that scare.

It was a scare. Primordial monsters sunk
in psychic muck, goose-necks alert, teeth honed
sharp as axons, begin to rise
dividing waters and vapors, shaking the earth
at the first sign. *Mother's* their latest favorite
but *touch* has always been a sure thing.
To live with grace *and* monsters—to be Loch Ness,
hold monsters landlocked and undersea, permit
only the rare surfacing and that against my will—
requires a soul of infinite fortitude
and uncommon beauty. Mine, though brave, has grown
grotesque at last through living so much with monsters.
Take the old bugaboo physical contact
for instance; it keeps great power over me.

I cannot kiss my good calm friend
simply—must uproot hills, blow cornets, make
a Gesture, a Claim:
"Mother is how I feel!" And *mother* and *touch*
touch off their queer commotion below. Snaky heads lift,
great hulks stir, water pours darkly
down massive shoulders and legs like trees; in another moment
they'd have been loose in this kitchen, and what I feel
is the blue weakness of panic.

And what I want, for now, is to be gathered
Against her girth, into her body's heat
And smell, and feel her pulse, unshaken, beat
As though this act were usual, be mothered
Just as I am—old, gangling, and grotesque—
Till calm and warm; and that
Often as I want. Oh, it's too much to ask

Of anyone, of life itself; I don't.
Think what it means to own so queer a wish,
To be self-orphaned, unsufficed by flesh,
And full of sluggish blood! Think if a Saint
Bernard, or Shetland pony, say, should plump
Its rank, unseemly crush
Of body in one's lap—legs, hair, tongue, rump,

And all, and paw and kick the very breath
Out of one! Yes, for I am like that too,
Even to myself. Who'd take *me* on? Would you,
Would she, would anyone who guessed the truth?
My sump of monsters gripes my belly, awake,
Fretful; and just so
Must monsters fret in many another freak

Who craves in his besotting famine of need
Not the womb merely, nor the perfect lay,
But something like a lap, forbidden. May
All freaks and cripples feed
At times, against all hope, at the breast. Dear friend
Or mother, it was queer Walt Whitman who said
That touch was about as much as he could stand.

1    The conversation has gone not at all badly.
     We have sautéed the mushrooms
     Poured out the plastic flask by amber fractions
     And here at evening's far end
     Brace to negotiate an awkward synapse,
     Your departure. Grin stiffening, I am canted
     Against the kitchen table, where in a few seconds
     My nerve will snap; you stand. Your smile
     Divides a slight flush under spikes of hair.

2    Our silhouettes, flung fuzzily over the sealed
     Door, waver. Mine wavers most. "Well, my dear,"
     You say turning to me—and that is when we hear
     The small snapping sound. Next, mouth brightly congealed,

     I seem to be unlatching the door, which grows
     A black border. Rain-pungent spring night blows
     In. While our smiles smile madly away, your eyes
     Under the cocked brows of mild surprise

     Glitter from mine to the latch and back again,
     Seeing doors blown shut no doubt as well as the one
     Opened. You are amused! Abruptly then
     You grasp my cold hand—go at once—are gone.

Waking I cannot piece my dream together.
In minutes everything is lost
But sweetness, and one scene. Making the bed
With tender gestures I add to the old list.
I knew this time you were a man.
We moved along a sidewalk, in the sun,
And you began
To pivot round me, turn and dance,
Drawing your slow hand
Around my collar. I draw a shaky breath, brim-
Full with the simple sunny love of the dream.

A clay cup am I, filled clear to the brim.
You are my saucer of silver, you must not
With tea, tears, anything, I must never
Wet you, you must not be wet.

*Seiurus aurocapillus*. Field marks:—5½–6½. A
voice in the woods. A sparrow-sized ground War-
bler of the leafy woodlands. . . . The bird is usually
seen *walking* on pale *pinkish* legs over the leaves
or along some log. It is *heard* a dozen times to
each time seen.
        Roger Tory Peterson, *A Field Guide to the Birds*

With fantastic care my feet laced up
in thick oiled boots with B. F. Goodrich soles
crush ripple patterns into the leaf-mulch. Stop.
Leaf fibers crumpling almost noiselessly
might spook him now: stand still.
Again *chertea'*  he sings,   CHERTEA'  CHERTEA'
an airy vessel seems to fill,
grow heavier, shatter; still his tree conceals
the Oven-bird. The Oven-bird is shy.

My 7 × 35 field glasses, which beat
their heartbeat rhythm against my chest
through all these mornings, like a mirror or pool
have filled with images: thrush, chat, waxwing,
song sparrow, indigo bunting, yellow-throat.
And, as they hold on a call,
the daub in a tossing sapling leaps into focus, breast
streaked rich brown and white,
again flings up his open beak, and shuddering
with effort, sings where I can watch him sing.

But the secretive Oven-bird never blooms
in their field. Over fallen leaves he comes,
he goes, a dozen times is heard
for each time sighted:  *tea'*  CHERTEA'  CHERTEA'
—and never, never by me,
though I search for pink legs walking a rotted stump
always, and often hear him. Even as I clump
my clumsy shoes once more toward his tree
I know I shall not see the Oven-bird.

Having vowed never again to be your guest
Three years past, atwitch with wryness today
I sit beside you and secretly rehearse
Old grievances. Not coming back made sense.

You speak of your father, after the divorce
Seen seldom, never close. Just as you say
Why you paid the strains and silences it cost
To be near him, things dissolve in radiance.

II

DEERFLY    Winged sizzling pellet am I
and mottled flat triangle. Shrieking
blood-lust animates me as Soul
Body her pupa. My meal is the thin pain
where your hair divides in oil, my life a headlong
hurtling upon crowns of heads—your own
succulent head, the huge hard
unswishable heads of horses. You are wrong
to hate me; if I torment you
that is my doom.

MOSQUITO    I am all thin: subtlety on a thin
whine, six cocked legs hair-fine;
your skin where they touch down
is thicker. I am all
pin-striped, pin-slender, head
a perfect pinhead, mouth whose tiny puncture
can slip between nerveends more needle-
sharp than any pin. Sweat
is my Siren scent, my greed is boundless
witless and impersonal, my nature
none of my choosing.

TOGETHER    O to turn aphid! O
for unresistant leaf-juices and no
murderous mammoth hands whacking! Never to be
tangled again in hair or spotted on your wrist
sipping, and no chance for a getaway.
—Though you knock ME senseless a dozen times—
—Or flail *me* away —what can we do
but sort our wings and legs and try again
again and yet again? Starve or be slapped to death
is what it comes to. Pity us:
the thirst for blood is a curse.

I found one fall snugged tight onto its twig
A tapered swelling spun, a woven chamber
Milkweed-pod shapely, roughly half that big,

And like a pod which has by late September
Split open, spilt its cottonseeds and dried
To wrapping-paper lightness. Was this slumber?

A death? The chamber seemed unoccupied
And much unraveled at the tip, though shaken
It rattled as if *something* were inside—

A walnut in its hull . . . I'd touched the broken
Skyblue or speckled cups of songbird eggs
And shells of locusts, each a hollow icon

Still clinging to the bark with empty legs,
And loved their one-time tenants' winged completion;
And, knowing well what fragile sorts of dregs

Cicadas, sparrows, seeds leave, my impression
Of this cocoon's light dryness kept me quite
From seeing any signs of occupation.

And that was why, one January night,
I jerked awake for such a ghostly reason:
Somewhere I'd heard the thumping-flopping flight

Of wings shut up in darkness and in prison,
Doggedly feckless. Hangers crashed and clanged
Another terrifying diapason.

I lay a long time while the trapped wingsbanged
Themselves on wood and wire in their trouble
And blindly ricocheted and boomeranged

And flop-thumped till exhaustion wore them feeble
Inside the only closet in my room.
And when I switched a lamp on and felt able

To open it
                there toppled from the gloom
Heavily sideways, stunned by light, a glory
Huge as a plate, with tiny perfect plume-

Like new antennae, feet red-orange and furry,
Thick furry abdomen, each panting wing
Powdered with cocoa-colored plush and starry

With one rich eyespot. Months before the spring
The furnace warmth had brought him forth in splendor,
Mad with an urge that powered his battering:

*Break free and find your mate O find her find her!*
My windowsills lay inches deep in snow
The females meant for him were sleeping under.

Born out of season, twenty years ago.
The wasteful barren death of so much beauty
Should hurt me till my own. I've come to know

Too well since that cold night in Cincinnati
What barren is, and for my sorry crime
Begun to know a terror and a pity

Unsayable save through this keeping time,
These saving graces slanted rhyme and rhyme.

*Flurry*

Going south along Mexico 15, near the Pacific,
We drove into a flurry of butterflies erratically
Westbound. We held the road and our speed, while butterflies
Came filtering through shoulder shrubbery, died violently
Upon the windshield, died in the radiator,
Or wavered across intact by the tens of thousands
And sifted into shrubbery leaves again.
The open windows snatched butterflies; we shut the windows
So they began in streaks to die. Flying
They looked white, but captives and casualties were pale,
Pale green-yellow, small and frail
And in no way remarkable
Individually. We traveled so for hours,
Colliding with butterflies, while great pastel
Multitudes flew over, lilting and fluttering,
While the air moved white with little wings,
Scraps of dusty muslin, beating toward the sea.

Always when I'd observe
White Admirals greedily
swarm and cluster
over still-warm clotted
horsedung, my mind
like the snob it pretends
not to be would frame
in *mots* its strong sense
of the ironic and the
alien. But one afternoon,
crossing a valley between
two ranges, I sighted a
fledged family of Mountain
Bluebirds, the males'
backs and all their wings
and tailfeathers flashing
the exact incredible
shading-into-turquoise
hue of the sky just deepening
toward autumn. Swift-
or Swallowlike they seemed
caught up in a family
frolic over a black pond
in a pasture, earthen
banks trodden all round
to muck evidently by
hoards of ponderous
thick things with split hooves
and casual habits.
The pond had a floating
cataract, and stank. And
close then high above it
seven sky-blue Bluebirds
swooped! banked! swooped! but
never quite dabbled
the surface of that standing
water too dull to mirror
the dyepot sky
or themselves dipping up,

deep in and out again: ah,
even to me—and I've
no patience with
anthropomorphizing—it
looked like play . . . much later
I awoke to the long time
I'd stood watching, and the
lone blue thought flying in my mind, envious, wordless.

## BLITZ

This morning, dived on by a hummingbird
While ambling from the washhouse, blind with sun,
Far from the city, worshiping the word,

I blessed the summer writing grant, conferred
To put me on this mountain where I've been
This morning dived on by a hummingbird.

Scant inches from my scalp the sharp wings whirred,
Sheer motion, visible though mostly seen
Far from the city. Worshiping the word

I worshiped also him and his absurd
Attack when I trespassed through his terrain
This morning. Dived on by a hummingbird

At seven, chilled, sun-blind! The brightness blurred,
Stung; and now I from his electric green
Far from the city, worshiping the word,

And holy words compound these verses—stirred,
Glad, grateful for the mountain's earliest boon
This morning, dived on by a hummingbird
Far from the city, worshiping the word.

## GIRL SCOUT CAMP VILLANELLE

For the Campers and Staff at Lazy Acres,
San Isabel National Forest, Colorado

> *Ego sum pauper.*
> *Nihil habeo.*
> *Cor meum dabo.*

Here in these mountains nothing else is real.
The very aspen leaves grow heart-shaped here.
They say what matters is the way I feel,

And quake to dramatize how slight, how frail,
How fearful in their mindlessness they are
Here in these mountains. Nothing else is real.

Pity the Penn State intellectual
Awake beside a thirsty, shambling bear!
To say: "What matters is the way I feel"

While, shadow on the tent's thin canvas wall,
He coughs and sways through lantern-light, so near!
Here in these mountains nothing else is real

Save feeling, and my twenty Scouts who shrill
Their Latin round, lit faces toward the fire,
Would say what matters is the way I feel

About them. They will give their hearts if I'll
Give mine, that yammers like a squirrel with fear
Here in these mountains. Nothing else is real,
I say; what matters is the way I feel.

## WASH IN EIGHT COLORS
*Logan River, Utah*

Clear sheets of water, sliding over stones
By deepening water-colors glorified,
Hold blue and green and something nearly bronze.

Though only ochre, khaki, several tones
Of raw and burnt sienna cobble wide
Clear sheets of water sliding, over stones

Trees marching up Earth's cracked, enormous bones
Stiffly in tiers, sky ceiling waterslide,
Hold blue and green; and something nearly bronze—

Reflective—happens when the sunlight hones
The surface like a knife. If willows hide
Clear sheets of water sliding over stones,

Or they opaquely stumble onto zones
Less candid, then those shallower sheets, stone-tied,
Hold blue and green and something: nearly bronze

One breath, the next clear water whirls, seethes, groans,
Turns frost-white. But the instant stones subside,
Clear sheets of water sliding over stones
Hold blue and green and something nearly bronze.

Like other powerful and difficult friends
mountains can be temperamental. In late
summer a daily crisis comes upon them. However
bluely benign their dawns, on any August afternoon
it's a question of when, not whether, to expect
the colossal tantrum. Each day's set problem
is to predict when that unpredictable temper will
break, blow rain, rain blows—second-guess
if the fluff behind Electric Peak's brown
tonsure of lichen cinquefoil scrub and scree
will have shown its true colors and proportions
by one o'clock, or not till six. No calm before
the storm. Climbs chanced early require of climbers
vigilance, nimbleness—   Off now? Then pay attention:

Glance at the sky constantly, keep constantly
straining to hear if every low noise was just
a jeep or plane, or another detestable trail bike, or
the mountain's muttered "Turn back!" which only a fool
would disregard. Risky, in August, even to rest
long beside any watercourse above trickle-size,
since all sounds—birdsong, grasshoppers' clacking,
the first soft belly-rumble of thunder—are drowned
in a stream's downpour of sound. By the time thunder
claps louder than loud water, or you craning over
a shoulder can see the heart-stopping oilsmoke-grey
thunderhead shove its streaky smudged leading edge
swiftly over the tall peaks, straight at the sun—
make no mistake: your very life's in danger.

Leave that high country fast then, get well
below the perilous summits and ridges lightning
loves and strokes fervently and would blast you from
with no more malice or compunction or even
consciousness than yours should one lug of your bootsole
be set on a black ant sometime during your
scrambling-stumbling forced retreat on knees gone
rubbery with the fright and fighting gravity
down down and down, three miles of steep stony
trail twisting from timberline to trailhead
through the cold dark. Though afterwards mountains
remember no grudge and will welcome you as warmly
as ever, learn now that to blunder in high places
when the manic fit overtakes them is to court death.

Long view: serried Spruce trees have spiked the slope
perhaps to bedrock; wherever they've left rifts
at ragged random, lightheaded Aspens sweep
downcanyon, filling the vast cleft in drifts
the shape of snow. Like Bible leaves their leaves
let light through, turn. Green froth more yellow than blue,
yellow threatens all summer to break through
then does, marbling the mountain like a cake.
*Giddy things.* The Spruce forest disapproves
deeply, more blue than yellow, constant, opaque.

Closeup: on needle bottle-brushes a bloom
of plum-bloom blue: Blue Spruce. Just at the crux
of turning, a single Aspen might display
two sweet Life Saver colors, lemon and lime,
on two limbs. Wind, for which that Aspen shakes
its loose crown like a pitchforkful of hay
and speaks like water flowing, leaves the Spruce
unmoved, holding their ground from scalawags—
gentleman soldiers brought to Daphne's pass
by way of the playing fields of Eton. *Prigs.*

The bark of Aspens, yellow-greygreen-green
variously, feels smooth and cool as skin
between knots, rings, and deepdown parallel
gashes scratched by a claw-sharpening bear
who drops his blueblack scat to sign the trail
after the treetrunk with a gruff "Keep off.
Et ego in Arcadia." Up here
no snowdrifts; foliage leaf by single leaf
hangs overhead, thin-whetted double blades
of a hard glitter, the slope's long suit of spades.

Singly responsive also to the least
breeze-breath, each blade twirls on a petiole
*flibbertigibbet* scribbling its light namesake
tremor on wind. They might seem jungle bamboo—
these straight pale shafts, this thicket closing the beast
with honebark claws—if Aspen leaves spoke Frond.
Stiffly above them all, pretending to
ignore wind's blandishments, the Spruce hold still
untouched unyielding *frauds* and sign the wind
a way the deaf and blind could not mistake.

Now whatever I glimpse qualifies the vast
disc whose rim is the horizon. Past
cornfields rumpling to the world's edge
and over, past haystacks shaped into

great coarse-grained breadloaves,
I am driving alone across Nebraska. I
in my midget car am the circle's moving
center, the whole horizon slides west

with me as the highway slides under,
soil off a moldboard. Bicycle pince-nez
glinting, one aluminum camper after
another swings around me, outrageously

exceeding the dream-slow fuel-poor downward-
adjusted speed limit. My car, blue dot
humming through the trackless mirage-slow
sea of grass's memory, steadily

exceeds the speed limit by so little
no cop could possibly care, and passes only
the fixed things I-80 ruts and gouges
itself among: wheatfields; beetfields;

old homesteads the first sodbusters built
soon as they could pay for lumber
hauled overland from the Missouri,
each house, barn, outbuilding

in its cottonwood windbreak rooted
against the right hunch of land long calm
decades before the Federal plowboy
leaned to his task. Their fitness here seems

absolute, but the contoured concrete furrow
curves at the doorstep now. I know, I always
know, that when I kill my pounding engine
at every halt for tea, the perpetual

wind, blind and baffled, too ancient
to change her ways, still will be ruffling
the highway's beautiful shoulder-length
thatch of blond weeds.

1    AUGUST / YAKRICKS

Past our train's sliding window flick odd headless herds
Of hayricks, shaggy-pelted
As gaunt yaks. Spry little oxpeckers of birds
Rummage the pastured flanks so brownly abristle,
Several to each unaccountably thatched and stilted
"Rhino." How rough these beasts, how docile,
How . . . *regimented* into precise square-angular
Spacing and stance: wooden feet hid stock-still
In grass, wooden bones under that stiff hair
Profusely sunning! Sometimes, while the rails slope
Alongside, every yak-backbone points downhill,
Which grazing Guernseys are known or supposed to do.
But a *cow* would switch her hard frayed-rope
Tail at the sparrows, moo,
Jostle.

2    NOVEMBER / THE MEDUSA BIRCHES

In a Bergman screen set that looks to be nationwide
Emphatic conifers do not, as you might expect,
*Exhaust* like the bald birch shafts upended and pricked
Into the tan pincushion of the countryside,
A currycomb bristle it hurts my scalp to see

Thin reddish branches frizz the white glare of poles
Over, poles and branches contriving to imply
Innumerable unseen mouths, rounded black holes
Below innumerable arms flung straight at the sky. . . .
"Astonished?" Exactly. Flung up in astonishment.
Many thousands dense they gesture three sides around
The fields of strawstack gnomes hunched on the bare ground
Disheveledly; crowd stark and gaunt
Along both banks of the rivers where stouter logs
Swim south corraled in shoals; elbow to stare
Shocked upon the slaughterhouse lumberyards where
Others lie peeled and piled. Above the thin fogs
Above the marshes, frantically perpedicular,
The arms signal alarm. Winter trains have passed
Hourly between these groves of eerie sentinels,
A clacking lurching line of windows and wheels;
The birches stand there perpetually aghast

making their voiceless indignation a cry
visible as the visible click of trunks
moving on one another    tilted this way
the painted clownface grins that way it winks
dodging behind some vertical black lines
on a plastic square    I cannot number
his postures as the guttering wood aligns
in the trainwindow's frame    pale stripes of timber
I cannot positively make out the clown
whom death could chalk no whiter than his cage
bars    pickets    playpen grille    rooted each in umber
upstreaking milk on snow    dull blush under beige
and struck
                    "to stone."

3    DECEMBER / DANCING-DAY PERSPECTIVE

> "Sing O my love, O my love, my love,
>   My love;
>   This have I done for my true love."
>           —*traditional English carol*

Cordwood, weeds, fences, meringued firs heel
On pasteboard props; New-England-looking boulders, grayed
Or blued by an early sundown which is real,
Lump in the foreground (chickenwire, papier-mâché'd)
Of the frieze of birch groves delicately scratched
Behind them with . . . a sapphire. Narrow white trail
Kinking through dark woods makes a negative
Of Nature like one July storm that pastiched
Earth, sky, and windblown daylight topside-flat:
Grass sallow, working clouds the color of slate
Clapped over it like a shell.

So winter, sheared from *Ideals* with a razor blade
In dry iambics and made a pin-out of.
Past this same window O my love, my love
Each glazed weed in that vast confection of fakes
Rears its individual stalk, the sprayed
Fir seedlings, blurred and pallid, reel from the tracks,
The stones sail backwards, humping their snowy backs.

# Litany

*for Anna and Harlan Hubbard*

### I PARABLE

In shoreplants on the teeming pond
A something pokes its nose through scum,
Cork-small, cork-bouyant. Reaching from
The boat I ambush with one hand

A painted turtle, dollar-size.
He scrabbles on my palm in dread,
His tiny old-man's neck and head
Outthrust and bobbing as he tries

To struggle free, to paddle quick
Beneath the scarf of lily pads
That hides him when the heron wades
Out after frogs and turtles: thick,

Cool, tangled, safe from heavyweight
Manhandling man—in whom, as in
This baby's shell and skeleton,
Man's chemicals accumulate.

While he—beguiled green swimming stone—
Through vegetation dives and floats
A sinister endowment waits
Embedded deep in marrowbone,

In belly-plates and turtleshell.
His automatic, scuttling feet,
Immersed, released, wigwag him straight
For cover. Down he goes. Farewell,

Small diver, camouflaged in flowers
Safe from my clutch if not my kind.
No one at all is safe; the wind
Blows poison in this pond of ours.

2    SUMAC

Bloodiest upon fall's deep flesh-tones, look
how sumac glows lamplike with the light
behind it! Stoplight green / yellow / red (red's
what glows) leaves clasp the same tree
loosely now, furred stems readily pull free.
Shaggy behind them irregularly rise maples
pin oaks and rich fruitcake-colored sweetgums, all
alight as if for traffic: but this dry rust-
russet mixed with light is of all most,
although not latest, nor quite longest, red.

3    DIRGE FOR SMALL WILDDEATH

So many damp hanks of hair and feathers
horribly take the measure of my country
walking: possums, grasshoppers, snakes,
frogs and woodchucks and sparrows, overtaken
by traffic, flattened or knocked aside.
Immense, our incidental slaughter
of small wild creatures. Today
I found another skunk, mouth full
of dirt, bloated, pregnant, dead
on her back. The pavement's smeared
with violent matted fur and entrails. A faint,
lingering, unmistakable skunk-musk
clings to the road's shoulder.

Bred wise enough to crouch
or scuttle from a man on foot
loose in their territory, what beguiles
these bodies new each morning
beside roads, when they in safe darkness
emboldened by their stink
come trotting out of brush thickets
onto the hard surfaces where huge
blinding things rush upon them? What
can it mean to luckier skunks
to happen on this one: food for nothing,
defending no kits, not starved, diseased, tooth-torn,
trapped by water or fire—yet dead?

## 4 EVENSONG

Now the Earth turns, and tilts me from the sun.
Her swirling whites and blues grow shadowy now.
Twilight. Then dusk. Soon night must fall, a crow
Sweeping strong feathers down.
This lovely leper Earth, so lovely still
She stops the heart, will never, now, get well.
Her sluggish stinking rivers flow to oily
Seas; her skies, stack-tortured, thicken daily.

Above me now—far, high, outstripping sound—
A jet's thin parallel emissions shine
Roseate with the sunset's benison;
Soften; and pillowlike are plumped by wind.
The little silvery thing,
Wasp-graceful, tilts its warheads on one wing
And turns as Earth does. Steady and serene
It draws the spreading threads out in a line.

And nearer carrion crows than this are circling
The Earth in torment. Men of Power aggress,
Plunder, wrest, blast, enkindle furnaces
And manufacture things. Our desperate darkling
Globe cannot be healed except through power;
For Progress and the GNP therefore,
Leisure, and General Prosperity,
The Earth shall surely die.

She is a living sacrifice that saves
Nothing. And though the stopwatch heart be struck
Dumb with Earth's beauty still, I see the wick
Shorten, the flame flicker. Red lancet leaves
Hurtle against my heart, against blue sky;
Now by that piercing, deepening blue I swear
To cherish life, while round me, vivid, pure,
Life licks and burns at me.

5    WHEN PROFITS RISE
      (PRAYER ABOUT AN INVESTMENT)

I am a busy man, O Lord,
My time's been hard to buy
Since I made Chairman of the Board;
Yet here in church am I.

My new clock-radio jolted me
Awake at seven-fifteen.
I scrubbed my teeth electrically,
My shaver stroked my chin.

The juice whirled in the blender while
The electric coffeepot
Reheated last night's Yuban. Well,
I drank some scalding hot;

Loaded the four-slice toaster full
Of frozen waffles; ate;
Then donned this dark expensive wool
And drove to service late.

Next Thursday is Thanksgiving, Lord,
And richly hast Thou blessed.
This family can now afford
To worship with the best.

Since last November we've acquired
The power boat, the Ski-doo,
A fourth TV, a car (our third),
An intercom, a new

Dishwasher, and extension phones
For all the kids. I guess
I keep up with that bastard Jones!
But if I'm a success

I know Whose blessing helped me rise.
"Man reapeth what he soweth."
Our nation of free enterprise
And exponential growth,

My ceaseless labors, and Thy love:
To each of these I owe
My earthly treasure; so I give
Thy Church the cut it's due.

That's first good business, plus it's fair:
When profits rise, I make
Damn sure this outfit gets its share,
With thanks. For Jesus' sake . . .

PRAISE GOD FROM WHOM ALL BLESSINGS FLOW
PRIASE HIM ALL CREATURES HERE BELOW
PRAISE HIM ABOVE YE HEAVENLY HOST
PRAISE FATHER SON AND HOLY GHOST

Amen.

6    MUMMY BAG

a lifemask of chill morning
fits me    through warmth I burrow
toward waking    over and over
towhees pronounce their names
I hooded in feathers lie
zipped to the chin in feathers
the strengthening sun tightens
rope and canvas around me
filled suddenly with wind
the tent lifts like a sail

7    ARMADA

On poured cement shall break the sea
At Provincetown, at Wilmington;
The beaches plovers step alone
Beneath one concrete slab shall lie,

Bleached of its fine bluegreen-and-umber
By poured cement and diesel smoke
From Salem south to Roanoke.
The land shall neither sleep nor slumber

Till Stonington, Connecticut
To the numbed wave descend supine,
A concrete laprobe rimed with brine
Where once her teeming tidal flat

Brimmed and was windblown. And the sun
Shall feebly etch, through hydrocarbs,
That afghan's zigzag cracks and curbs
Where roller-skating children spin

In Stonington with pearl-gray faces.
Then from this seaboard west shall roll
The trucks whose guts, a churning hole,
Are full of gray and gritty feces

Which do not fuel but petrify
The living soil they overspread.
The trucks' advance shall leave it dead
Of paving. And its plants shall die,

And burrowing things, whose unimportant ghosts
Shall waver to and fro
Dimly above the superpatio
Between our ivory coasts.

## Instructions for Kindling Fire
## in a Wilderness

"Wherefore glorify ye the Lord in the fires."

—Isaiah 24:15

I    Prepare the ground: clear a rough circle
broad as a tall man of whatever
may be the least able to explode or burn—
flat stones, wood chips, tough brown grass.

Next, patiently find firewood. Refuse supple
wood and wood rotted at heart to powder,
save only what is best. Well-seasoned sticks
snap smartly when broken; testing as you go
halve some on a bent knee, lever
others underfoot, rap the heavy limbs
against a standing tree. Look up as well as
down: cast branches hang pronged among the living,
peeled pale in immolation.
All wood once lived. The decent trees
charitably give their bodies to be burned.

To your circle bring then in both hands
the tangles of what you have gathered.
Break slender antlered branches, use an axe
to split sawn logs and chop to length
the stoutest limbs, snap off small clutching
twigs. Measure wrist-thick fuel
near eighteen inches, thumb-sized kindling less,
tinder least. Grade
everything by girth, skinniest to stockiest.

Now you are ready.

II    Kneel. Fix in the circle's center
an A of medium kindling, crossbar upon star's point
firm. Against the bar on its open side, tilt
a tight fistful of twigs matchstick-size or slimmer.
Tinder should be bunched loosely
and placed so that a third of each twig's length
juts above the crossbar; unless supported well
it will burn through, like that!
and drop. Dried pine needles make excellent tinder
where pines abound, but you must learn how to select twigs.
Paper is profane.

III   Now abruptly, between one breath and the next,
feel your ring of bared earth become
the hub of the wilderness.
All round above you mountains, massive, cloven,
furred densely with green—blue-green
spikes of juniper, yellow-green sheen of maple—
will lean nearer and intense in their awareness of you
await the kindling of the fire;
expect this.

Use a wooden kitchen match. You will need only
one. Briskly scrape it aflame; cup its flaring; let it first
begin to char the stick, then
hold the match, low and burning,
beneath the sheaf of tinder. Hold it steady,
wait for the wisp of smoke . . . so. Wait
again. Then feed the spent match
to the red flower of fire and be there quickly
quickly with quarter-inch twigs.

This moment is crucial. Once alight
fire needs urgently to eat and breathe. You
must nurse it, judging from split
second to split second, throughout its quirking delicacy,
between wood and wind.
Feed it well, mindful that too many crowded
sticks will stifle a fire
so small born in still air. Breathe your own life
into it, blow yourself
lightheaded for fire's sake if you have to.

Slight tinder, ash
in seconds, has therefore only seconds
for persuading plumper twigs to burn, and those
may take but little longer to inflame
light kindling—it being the business of every
width to put the torch to a wider.
Mindful of air space, lay—
never fling—twigs and sticks
fanwise one by one against the A's by now smouldering

crossbar; stub larger ends on earth,
focus smaller above the infant
flame. Let each layer be well caught
before you add the next.
In this way arrange a kindling wigwam
tipped with fire, let it blaze; finally
box the wigwam in a cabin
woven of fuel and roof it flat with fuel, always
honoring by strict economy the lives of trees.

IV  Blue, orange, yellow, black and gray;
open eye, beam-full.

Where you crouch to stoke now and again
the licking wincing leaping shining thing
whose being you have wrought, with ceremony,
of heat and wood and air and this recipe has ceased
to be a hub. While you were busy
the wilderness accepted and forgot
you, the round altar, and the worthy fire.

# Two Poems

*After El Commendador Escriva's*
*"Ven, Muerte tan escondida"*
*as translated by*
*Henry Wadsworth Longfellow:*

Come, O Death, so silent flying
That unheard thy coming be,
Lest the sweet delight of dying
Bring life back again to me.
For thy sure approach perceiving,
In my constancy and pain
I new life should win again,
Thinking that I am not living.
So to me unconscious lying
All unknown thy coming be,
Lest the sweet delight of dying
Bring life back again to me.
Unto him who finds thee hateful,
Death, thou art inhuman pain;
But to me, who dying gain,
Life is but a task ungrateful.
Come, then, with my wish complying,
All unheard thy coming be,
Lest the sweet delight of dying
Bring life back again to me.

ECE / hwl

1    Come, O Death, so silent flying
On a sharp bright-feathered barb
Cast like bread upon the plying
Waters, wrapped in insect's garb.
Tear my horny lip; alighting
Delicately, make me strike.
Lure me, trick me. If you like,
Kill me. I shall come up fighting.
Life is good, but Death is better.
Though in rocks I live pell-mell,
Vivid through the pounding water,
Harmless, sleek, and powerful,
Hook me, hurt me, hurl my heaving
Gills to heave their last on shore.
Drowned in agony and air
Make me know I'm tired of living.
Drag me through my hour of dying
On a sharp bright-feathered barb
Cast like bread upon the plying
Waters, wrapped in insect's garb.

2    Come, O Death, so silent flying
Out of power plants, factories,
And the cars we can't stop buying.
To our dull collective nose
Waft the stink of our extinction.
Chink our blood and bones with lead.
Luxury's the bed we've made;
Bedded, grant us éxtreme unction.
(Will we get some? Does it matter?
Don't be troubled, don't be scared.
Life is good, but Death is better.
Mucking through this pile of merde
We'll die comfy; labor-saving
Gadgetry will help us stay
Soothed and happy. Anyway,
Weren't we pretty tired of living?)
Soar, then, choking, searing, drying,
Out of power plants, factories,
And the cars we can't stop buying
To our dull collective nose.

Calmly, breathing hydrocarbons,
the Holsteins my neighbors
amble from the barn
where steel fingers have milked them.
Their pasture freshens the moving
air; there at their leisure
they chomp the grass and there
with hoisted ropy tails
enrich it. They are virgin
mothers, each bred immaculately
with a glass vial. Rampant
ears of corn bursting
outrageously from the coarse
green thicket behind them
remind them of nothing.

And particles continually descend
upon cornfield and cowpasture.
They settle
softer than particulate snow.
The cows eat and inhale them; we all
do. They are part of us
as the tall stacks on the lakefront
are part of a landscape
which from their slope these cows
can see. They cannot see
DDT in white kernels, in tufts
of grass, in their own heavy
bones and leaded blood.

The cows accept everything.
Neither traffic, nor shoreline smog, nor
dark dust on the clover
seems ominous to them. A cow feels
*alive*, like life itself, not
self-aware. Her milk urges her
to the barn, her four stomachs to pasture.
Nearby, the jolly ithyphallic stalks
know ripening as the cows lactation
and hunger. What drifts
out of the sky, what climbs
their xylem tubes dissolved in rain,
are to them nothing. The tainted wind
stirs them, they send down
roots. Their fruit mellows secretly.

# III

1   In Sweden lakeshores and riverbanks
    Belong to nobody. Pierced by a glint
    Of water, any wanderer may freely
    Force passage through second-growth
    Birch or spruce and take the ritual plunge
    Without trespassing. Splashes
    Disperse in benign silence;
    In bone-cold solution, rust
    Tints pale skin like an eggshell.

    To each book or film its baptism:
    The eye dallies about thighs and calves
    Where blond hairs flatten as astream,
    Chests rising, rumpling wet heads,
    Vikings ascend to shore as from the half-
    Shell. The splendid buttocks of Max
    Von Sydow loom on the screen;
    Like an abashed turtle a penis
    Shrinks sweetly into print.

2   The blue knit tank suit being
    *De rigueur* at the YWCA, imagine
    My amazement! In our ship's pool
    Naked women were harrowing salt
    Water; others sweltered on sauna
    Shelves—heavy, pendulous, wholly
    Comfortable about their breasts
    And pubic hair. (As much could not be said
    Of two small playsuited voyeurs.)

    Nowhere among these bodies slick
    With candid sweat the casually
    Strategic draping of a towel,
    The arm's demure circumflex. Not
    Beautiful, nor proud, these women
    Had come to terms with something
    Elusive, hard to name. Instantly
    I knew it, and plunged with glee among them
    Into the sea-drawn shock of waters.

How quickly fondness runs
to flesh! Slow spangling palm-stroke warm
on the bare forearm,

brief kiss a brush-stroke on the face,
tight circling-and-release, slick thrumming
ultimate link—

one continuum
natural as breathing to the primitive
Kreën-Akrore hunters who slink then spring

splendidly naked through the Brazilian
rainforest, colored like copper or sand
under sun, and sleep

in a friendly tangle; but for us
garbed fallen ones, how alarmingly
with equal cadence

fondness runs to sin.

Skin
stringed instrument of affect fretted with nerve
is armor's plucky inverse

subversive by sweet nature, knowing
whose touch to sing to
only as the catgut-mellow guitar

knows. Strict homiletic insufferable
brain,
not skin, commands auditions:

"Fill out, please, this short application
fervently doublechecking in the squares provided
your true complete

responses as to *Marital Status Age* and *Sex*, also
one or two other critical
particulars, for which alas

skin never, never asks."

Never. Flushed slippery, skin basks
like plantain in strong
impartial sunshine. "Appropriate"

occurs nowhere in its pagan
vocabulary, all finetuned undertones and tremors.
In jungle heat begin

such sentimental journeys as can shiver
the Christmas-tree-globe
laws of Leviticus and of State

wholesale—not Faust's way
but the highpitched scream's;
their gibberish of splinters remotely rings

a lush green world. Inside
lively, delicate, willful as windchimes
sleek skin spreads leaflike

and flowerlike opens, and only to true suns.

Afternoons when the metal dock
burns and flashes like
a gunbarrel, unbearable
till splashed, and lake and sky,
different blues, both beautiful,
each has a sun in it
and the wet dock another
like an egg frying,
you and a few good friends
lug air mattresses along
and lie out on the brilliant
lake. Every so often somebody
flops off into that shocking
cold, and swims
a long way. In a little while
*you* take the plunge. You
heave out chilled through,
gasping, yet in no time
have drifted dry
save for random drops and warm
clear puddles trapped
in your own clefts and
hollows and your rubber
raft's. Nobody talks
much. No clammy
elasticized fabric clutches
you. Floating, you flush
evenly all over; soak up sun
like a drug; expand. Groggily
turn over. Grow drowsier
sun-logged
logy . . . Yelp and overturn.

Midnights when mist
billows thick as fog
off the lake, you and your
same friends whose bodies
you know so well have lit
the antique automobile headlamp
and shawled in towels
followed it the quarter mile
to the invisible
dock. Its furry beacon
alone marks the earth's edge.
Damp clothes clump there
waiting. You cannot
see them or each other
through opaque air marginally
thinner, paler, chillier
than the dense black
water. Above the headlamp's
hissing cut shrill
sourceless voices. Borne up
into one cold element
by thrusting into another, you
feel the places where
beam diffuses into then becomes
mist, misty sky
lake and lake land
indefinite. You feel
not drowsy at all.
One night like this—deep, deep—
something will roil
the inky waters, will begin
to rise. Some other swimmer.

When I was six like
spring thaw a shallow
ditch bordered the back yard,
to probe whose fragrant black-
leaf muck and cornea of rain
with a wet stick excited

me unbearably. If ditch
were creek! its pointing
worms mere bait, its pools
kinetic with the lives
of crawdads, tadpoles,
snails and little snakes

striped like a stocking,
and *fish*! What *bliss*! How
do children come by what they
know? A cartoon movie seen
in school—a dragon, and
the prince that slew him

and married the king's daughter—
drove me to mass-reproduce
their scene of combat:
the little hero, the puny
hilted sword, the cave a gray
curve like a boulder, the slack

coils of the creature
sliding from the dark maw.
At the same age I drew,
fascinated, one after another,
families of snakes whose
loops and waves roundly

scrawled the rock grottos
in which (I believed) snakes
lived. All my drawings
were identical, done for the sake
of shaping snakes, not thereafter
to keep them shaped.

Timid, sheltered, a child,
how did I know? Know
how to be drugged on musky
water and leaves soaking
in water; how, seeing one dragon
once, utterly to say Yes?

The viewers' lamplit grins affirm
a comic likeness. My brother, shuffled somehow
between townscapes, emerges ironically
underexposed from the wall's gay
scrimmaging. In his arms he cradles
our spayed fat miniature dachshund, tenderly
swaddled in a teatowel, eyes bright wet, sharp
nose upturned. Little, he used to say
and mean it: "This dog is the one girl I like."

She is the only being he touches now.
His life precludes imagination;
moist lips, nipples, a lace-veiled crotch—all
the props of fancy's dreariest skinflicks—
strike *him* as visionary. Over and over
they smut his sheets, prod at his clinched
and cleated fly behind cushion,
shirttail, merciful magazine, whatever
comes to hand quickest. He is seventeen.

Girding up their own interesting neuroses
my friends' smiles glance about the dark room
The next slide
jams. My brother and the fat bitch
reappear and are at once
twisted to whorls shiny as though viewed
through tears. When the timbered
buildings resume and the street scenes
we are all relieved.

# Biology Lesson

The wet glass of cover-slip and slide
sandwiches a world. Spiraling
blunt creatures live in it
whose beating cilia outstrip
thick thumbs that orbit them from side to side
under a colossal eye.

"The Paramecium's Sex Life"! Ordinary
fission—anticlimactic thing,
a latitudinal split
athwart that homely length of lip
the "buccal groove"—comes later and is very
ordinary.

But first these beasts, dumb, unicellular,
mindless, achieve by blind desire
what we who speak and think
must fight for: two by two they press
their buccal grooves together; then each pair
exchanges nucleoplasm.

An even swap: one animal gives up part
of itself and gets an equal share
of the other one. The link
breaks after this, the deep long kiss
unseals. So fortified, they separate
each to its schism.

I    At the intersection he'd picked for it—
     six lanes of traffic and a thick crowd on foot—
     the island of concrete made a natural stage
     perfect but for the whipping
     snow and probable police, and plainly
     he was past caring. His was a need

     Not Done in any weather, if least
     in a blizzard, but he was past caring
     about that too; he had to take us by storm—had
     to make us see his simple tableau
     for ourselves. There were hundreds badly
     jolted at the sight of that

     bizarre yet classic pose: coat open, pants agape,
     hairless pink sensation poked
     nervily into the frigid light and somehow
     managing, despite twenty bitter
     degrees of frost, to hold its own. The offender's
     bare slipnoose of finger and thumb

     kept up tender attentions. Jovial,
     cordial, high as a kite, he rocked on run-over heels;
     he aimed for the *best* exposure. One shouting
     arm-flapping constituent shared
     his cement soapbox—but no mere outrage
     could cow him now he'd made it that far.

II   And of the hundreds, only that lone critic
     hung around. For everybody else it was be hit
     and run: one look of pure horror, then a panic
     rout against the light, eyes fixed on feet and slush,
     from surer deadlier peril. And my own
     moment on the fantastic isle

     was no exception, I scuttled away
     slick as a cockroach. What might otherwise have
     become of me? How many also heard a deep
     chord struck from a keyboard, a key slip
     deep in a lock? For though we lack daring and well know
     how many hearts' desires are Done,

we fled undreamed-of selves each swollen
with envy, lusting all at once to stand
where three roads meet, rip decency's codpiece off
howling *Look! Look!* and ram down all those
delicate throats and be damned! How many of us
struggled not to brandish forth

some hard truth: "People don't respect me, I'm scared
all the time," or "When I touch my wife I can feel
her flesh crawl. Not a one of the kids is mine."
Sham, shame. Whatever.
The one home truth most private, most
unspeakable, hardest and truest. That very one.

A double city block of valuable real
estate once grazed by cattle here declines.
Gray buildings close it in. Collecting trash
it lolls in squalor. Self-absorbed machines
ride fence around it, and loose herds of ash-
hued pigeons, grimy sellout city fowl,
trek through its frayed grass. Starting witlessly
here, there, another place, they peck-peck-peck-
at popcorn, bread cubes, filter tips, the whole
drab throng in concert; a toy wooden chick
weighted upon a paddle of old brown wood
pecks *it* that way. Benched voyeurs often spy
a cock that all at once begins to scrape
the grass with stiff tail-feathers, muscular neck
flexing. Gargling endearments, he tails a hen
fanatically absorbed herself in food,
bustles and swells in her oblivious wake
and does his level best to stage a rape
but can't keep her positioned right—and *then*,
abruptly losing interest, strolls away,
great gular pouch deflated, crest fallen slack!
I bear in mind, when those perennial rakes
who prowl the Green approach my book and me
through the grim sunshine, trousers spiked with sex
for my sake, the abstracted pure reflex
of pigeons.

"Last night . . . the festival took on a new smell
and a new dimension when girls, presumably
from the Women's Liberation Front, invaded the
auditorium. Bob Hope was performing his rou-
tine cabaret turn when a sound of rattles and dis-
turbances diverted attention to a group of girls
rushing down one of the aisles, sprinkling papers
as they went. Sixty seconds' noisy, smelly pan-
demonium reigned."
                                  —Manchester *Guardian*

The 58 girls in spike-heeled pumps will clop
a steeplechase of steps and planes.
Their coifs are great stiff clots of spray.
They have oiled their exposed skins
like distance swimmers, they all have suited up.
Now for their countries and the BBC

58 flaming mouths on stilts will pace,
pose, pivot, effortfully grin,
askewing dry thick masks of face,
their neat enamel nothings at the cameramen,
and on a chalkline queue.

Miss Denmark and Miss Colombia confess
they're models to a microphone; Miss South
Africa, who wants to buy a minidress
in London, works as a mannequin; and, yes,
Miss France is a model; so's Miss Israel,

who couldn't look less Jewish and is blonde.
They may be beautiful, it's hard to tell,
but each seems package-perfect and well wound
up, excepting only Miss Yugoslavia, model, who'll
hang her heel in a minute and though 58th
scurry to her stanchion the long, wrong way round.

But now a familiar spirit of such events
bounds in on cue, swoops into his routine.
His puzzled English audience
attempts politely to include
him in its genial mood . . .

abruptly, unbelievably, he's rattled down—
stinkbombs, flourpackets puff across his stage—
leaflet-littering the aisles he sees with rage
some Feminists, who wear levis and not bras!
Later the shaken emcee prophesies:

"Anyone who would do anything
against these marvelous girls must be
on some kind of dope,
ladies and gentlemen," says Hope,
and adds that there must come a reckoning;
Somebody Upstairs is going to make them pay.

No fear, sweet Bob. An audience adores
indignant righteousness; this one applauds,
endorses, cheers, is well and truly yours
at last; and you are decency's and God's
and everybody knows it! More, knows which

girls are the marvelous ones! Do they, B.H.?
Chuck the she-devils out, bring on the twits,
say one is Fairest Twit Of All. And then
tell us how pleased you'll be when life requites
the unlovely Libbers, who cry this beauty down.

# Mistress Hutchinson
## and the Establishment

Anne Hutchinson in 1637
Was brought to trial before the ministers
Of Boston. For her certain hope of heaven
And an unseemly forwardness of hers
To question clerical authority,
She stood convicted of the heresy

Called *Antinomianism*. Next to death,
The harshest sentence which the courts could mete
For crimes against the wholeness of their faith
Was banishment, and that was what she got.
An Indian tomahawk in '43
Stove in her skull in Dutch New York, where she

Had settled. Boston's rapt, uplifted eyes
Saw God's hand on the hatchet, smiting Sin,
But the true case is this: societies
All punish those who deviate, or break down.
In unity is strength; conform therefore
And prosper, or expect the massacre.

One Peter Bulkeley wrote of Anne: "The just
Vengeance of God, by which shee perishéd,"
Should plainly "terrifie all her seduc'd
Followers." Bulkeley might as well have said:
*Death is the meetest wage of deviation.*
Convinced the axe cleft Anne to her damnation,

His satisfaction toad-bloats on the page.
He takes such pleasure in the suffering
Of tough Anne Hutchinson! The *surest* wage
Is death, I know that much. For differing
One pays and pays; all heretics subsist
Prey to the tomahawk or analyst.

Which is as it must be. A culture has,
In self-defense, to clout or shrink the brain
It can't incorporate. When Lowell says
With sorrow and righteous rage for queer Hart Crane
That dopes and prudes withheld Crane's Pulitzer,
He's blaming things for being how they are.

1   She knew. The wife's voice,
polite and terrible, hurled steel
curettes, outlining me—
neither quite Fair dummy nor wholly
human, though there were nicks
and blood-runnels. Oh,
that was a bad time.
I had imagined it all too
vividly, cramping, eyeballing
black acrackle at two in the morning:
it was the nightmare, come.
A doomed subtraction
straw by straw of everything it still
might mean instead took days,
and in the end
left only "She smells a rat. Her
talk's too pointed," flat.

2   Curious that exposure largely
should mean relief. Out of that bag,
cat! If this is the death
of us you may as well un-
cramp first, tongue your fur flat,
and see the sun, and let the sun
see you. I'm fagged out, I admit it,
juggling twenty claws in a humping
gunnysack. Damn them,
they pricked through
not like conscience yet
at all the wrong times; times
were all wrong. Another curious
thing though about exposure:
it's lost her her advantage. I mean
somehow she needed me in the dark,
wondering.

3   Decency is left even to those
    who have lost everything
    else; one can still and always
    be kind. Charity may give
    shape to our grief and in any case
    we three are so like so many
    Virginia wounded in a Yankee
    field hospital where we ourselves
    come or no one does
    from cot to cot bringing water
    laudanum and lint. And charity
    serves also to keep one
    busy, which is not beside the point.
    *All* of us are losers, have lost
    yes everything but listen:
    this
    is as far as I go.

I was very angry. Somehow they always made me an-
gry. I know they are supposed to be amusing, and you
should be tolerant, but I wanted to swing on one, any
one, anything to shatter that superior, simpering com-
posure.
> —Jake Barnes in *The Sun Also Rises*

Each time I have a period—and that has only been
three times—I have the feeling that in spite of all the
pain, unpleasantness, and nastiness, I have a sweet
secret, and that is why, although it is nothing but a
nuisance in a way, I always long for the time that I
shall feel that secret within me again.
> —Anne Frank

The trouble with being a woman, Skeezix,
is being a little girl in the first place.
> —Anne Sexton

Hypnosis might exhume the lost imperative
juncture when I knew: *Everything*
*my mother is, that I must never be.*
What animal craft let me in on a verity
reason would not confirm
for years? This baffles me. By five
they said I walked like a farmer, informing
people when asked that I wanted to be "an artist
like my Dad" someday, though evidently I had
no skill but the copyist's, and drew
quite wretchedly from scratch. That cold
moody young man, my father, whom to have preferred
seems blasphemous still! Death's-head
will-o'-the wisps brewed deep in the bogs
and wastes of *her* acquiescent treachery
must have spooked me, settling for good
the choice I cannot remember which, willy-nilly,
do what I may, my gait cannot forget.

Bluejeans provoked a first seizure
of passionate desire. I would have done
anything, promised anything, to make the next blest
morning illumine their side placket healed
miraculously on the closet doorknob
into a zip front fly. My desperate prayers,
however, failed; each dawn's
panting investigation found the snug smug thing
unaltered. Some mothers buy boys'
jeans for a daughter? Not mine; neither God
nor coarse phenomenal cloth seemed as adamant.

Joe Gibson in my fourth-grade class
couldn't pronounce *th*. "My favver's dead,"
he'd say. "Round John Virgin, muvver and child,"
Joe caroled solo in a sweet
falsetto. He minced. Bigger boys
beat him up. I couldn't stand him.
My father observed with spurious logic:
"You don't like sissies, do you? Then why
act so much like a boy?" Frustration
made an aerosol bomb of me before his eyes!
*Unspeakable idiots* I thought, or felt
rather, utterly unable to express
my sense of criminal falseness in this
*whose maleness I so covet, thrown away,*
*wasted!* A decade older I would nod, hard,
at the stoppered outrage of Jake Barnes,
but things had changed. I've never been wholly
sure how to fathom the deep late wellspring
of my affection for homosexual men—unless indeed
being too akin under the scratched surface
I have no choice. Some of my best gay friends
wish me married or the safe side of sixty; we
unnerve each other. Empathy, envy, love:
troublesome gifts, all three.

How I admire (without being dogmatic
about it) men! Female bodies
do not offend me. But their shortcoming
is to lack, all, what I myself
lack, a thing worth envying, a fit object
even of worship: let the enormous lofty
phallus pass on its pole, I from my heart
will shout *hosanna*.
"Genitalia are homely but nice," someone said
meaning his own. Homely! Slack crowned cylinder
displayed sumptuously upon its cushion of balls,
warm, elastic, soft like a breast,
as benign to the cupping honorific palm until
attention goes to its head. Then feel it stir,
stiffen, stoutly project, a prodder
at length less admirable than entertaining,
less anything than urgent, mantled
Triceratops made flesh. To *look* at, though,
this connoisseur prefers them circumcised
and unaroused. As to color and size
no prejudice, little as to age.
The Greeks, whose fossil nudes and centaurs
struggle nowadays in London, knew
beauty when they saw it, and sculpted with love
the very horse-cocks in their scabbards.

*Women* are homely. The best-wrought
cunt is a dirty joke: intricate,
secretive, woefully without the simple cock's
clean outward shapeliness, seeping
perpetually, exasperating on cold
campouts *qua* plumbing device,
in short a bore. True: wired with nice
nerve-ends and relatively hard to hurt,
but beautiful? Never. Superb judgment
on somebody's part, to center
penis and testes in the limelight while
tastefully tucking their opposite number in.

At nine my traitorous body,
to my abject horror, bloomed.
Daughter of female generations

goat-udder buxom, I was doomed to cleavage:
to jiggle and swing through womanhood
though starved slim as a bicycle
handlebar. "You're just plain crazy,"
groused my father in a parody
of consolation, "that's what the boys
*like*. Lots of girls would give
their eyeteeth, etc." Oh sure. One woman I know,
having probably burned what she never needed
anyway, wears only soft knits and body shirts
against her skin. My hand would love
to smear across that moderate
roundness, as it loves soft organs
slung in jockey shorts and all full springing
human softnesses. But to this day
I loathe the C-cup harness I must cinch
around my own soft excess or never, on pain
of pain, run, dance, ride horseback. *Ladies
and gentlemen: the human form bovine.*

Coming down stairs
was torment in due time; that proud
flesh had acquired the swollen tenderness
of dead-ripe summer squash. Liquid
engorged each belly-cell. Something awful
was happening, I felt awful. "Mom, I'm *sick*."
"No you're not." "Then what's wrong with me?"
—Only Sex, only Life, just that I'd been sentenced,
given forty fertile years, to endure a full decade
toadlike with bloat, painbreasted; condemned
as well to shuffle through more than fifteen
months of individual First Days,
spine hunched weakly over my dumb blind
passionate fist of a womb's shuddering,
clenching, hot emptying of itself
nastily in shame and oh please God in secret . . .
(what blotty eighth-grade "accidents"—
so like, so miserably unlike
cracked voices and jack-in-the-box erections—
were to spill from that headstrong vessel
unmanageable at first as a green colt!)

Hysterical prisoner of Oestrus, my body
still spitefully revenges itself upon itself:
backache; fatigue; icy feet and hands;
digestive aberrations; and a dread
griping blunted only by much too much
antispasmodic / nervedeadener
clutched in whose complex alchemy
the heart flutters, jaw flexes,
face goes novocain-numb, and brain
squats in a muzzy languor. In drugs, nevertheless,
is all salvation. What did women *do*
before aspirin and phenacetin? Before laudanum?
Good God, what can they do
when the unstayable cycle claims them
despite revolutions, natural disasters, Auschwitz—
vomit and writhe in mud
for sixteen hours, skewered upon agony
more unremitting than labor's?

All this began for me, twelve years old,
in a Greyhound restaurant Ladies Room
beyond whose door my parents were putting
their heads together. Dad (gruff above
murmuring diners): "What are you looking
so embarrassed about? Do you think
you're the first girl it ever happened to?"
It had happened, I knew,
to Anne Frank and *her* father, and the *Diary* tells
she cherished as her "sweet secret" what I called
the Curse. Why, was the mystery.

Looking older than one's age required,
it dismayed me to learn, a decorum
appropriate not to the real but to the apparent.
Suddenly I must keep out of trees,
soapbox racers, unserious fights. The list
of harmless things no longer allowed
because I looked too old or was too old
or was not a boy lengthened, as did
the new list of recommended props
and capers: ballroom-dancing lessons,
sorority rush, lipstick, nylon stockings,
panty girdles, three-inch heels. An evil day
came when my father unfurled the future
he meant to clench for a daughter: he spurned
in anger, in contempt, and by the book as always,
some detail of house-drudgery as "women's
work," *ergo* fit for me and for my mother—
his scared, appeasing marshmallow-lieutenant
who accepted the humiliation, with a smile,
for both our sakes: "It's a man's
world." Those days, mad for survival,
I despised past all description being
a girl, despised girls that didn't, despised
and scorned girls who, like sissies
of whatever sex, ran and threw
a softball "like a girl," *i.e.* badly,
squealed, were squeamish, flirted. *Feminine*
would forever mean silliness and a limp wrist;
I'd not thought yet about *womanly*.

I    They gave me in my kindergarten year
     What seemed irrelevant, an Old Maid deck.
     Gems, wrinkled skin, strange glasses on a stick,
     Long gloves, pressed lips, and horrible orange hair,
     No child, no husband ever to be hers,
     That gaunt crone wasn't anything like me!
     I got her meaning fast: *ignominy*
     *Is being single in a game of pairs.*

     How could I have imagined singleness,
     Who called my mother's spinster aunt an old
     "Witch-widder" heartlessly and was corrected
     (A "maiden lady")? Nor had I suspected,
     A child myself, that yearning for a child
     Can raven even old maids like avarice.

II   Each morning of my tenth summer *swears Memory*
     *mythologizing as usual* our washer disgorged a pulpy heap
     of wet white strong cheap
     fabric, ropy, smelling of soap, which it was my
     job to untwist, shake out, nip
     onto the lines high in windy sun
     *it never rained* two corners to a clothespin,
     then prop still higher. *Flap*  Flap.

     I plucked them down
     stiffened, fragrant, mounding the basket knee-
     high, to be cleverly doubled to eight
     neat thicknesses by me each afternoon.
     Diaper service was costly, convenient Pampers yet
     to be invented. I was the diaper service. *Me*

III  Those were the clean ones, but I don't think
     I minded any of it;
     a fragrance must exonerate,
     somehow, a stink.

     I've sloshed hundreds of filled diapers in
     toilet bowls, not breathing;
     what I remember is a sheathing
     of powder on the changeling's clean skin.

And milkiness, patting his back
against my draped shoulder. For this, I see
the laundered airy diapers of Memory
peeling like lightning off the stack.

Not, not ever now, the crusty sour-
milk ones I very well know there were.

IV There had to be. Doctors: "Your baby has
pyloric stenosis," a valve constriction which meant
he threw up a lot. Eventually he went
back to the hospital and was dosed with drops.

My mother broke to me the fabulous news
she was "expecting" (at last! after the years of hopes
and disappointing miscarriages!) in the Maternity
Shoppe of a big downtown department store:

"What's a 'maternity dress'?" "For ladies to wear
while they're pregnant." "Who're *you* buying one for?" "Me!"

I used to say, back in the irresponsible Fifties,
I wanted "a big family." Though I was one of the tree-
dwelling, androgynous little girls dolls bore,
I always liked even upchucky babies.

V And all that windy, sunny diaper-summer—
His first, my tenth—I'd go out with our baby,
My little, little brother, walking. Maybe
His live weight on my heart induced the murmur
I always, lately, seem to hear. Returning
I'd feed him formula and sing, the rocker
Groaning a metronomic cadence, Shaker
Wisdom: *we come round right* I sang *by turning.*

Recalling what this battered snapshot shows,
The flannelette cocoon my sharp elbows
Bracket so bonily, a wash of joy
Transfigures all that gawkiness and spreads
Luminous circles right around both heads,
Mine, frowsy, and the fragile skull of the boy.

VI   so late as 65 a man has time   small
       wonder age obsesses   my own
       how inconceivably 31
       pelvis stiffening ova going stale

       Charlotte Brontë
       died at 39 of TB
       and the complications of a first pregnancy
       having it would have killed her anyway

       Eunice Kennedy Shriver
       handily started her large family at 32
       you don't know   can't know   you

       fret   you're apprehensive   terrified
       demons called mongolism and difficult birth invade
       your peace   *now* you conclude *or never*

Here is the first collection of a young writer acclaimed by Daniel Hoffman as "among the most accomplished as well as the most promising poets of her generation . . . able to hear and make us hear the felicities in formal conventions, which she uses as ways of defining her freedom."

The work is divided into three sections, the first dealing with ideas and people, the second with nature, the third with sex and being female. Judith Moffett writes free verse, but her book also includes a variety of received forms: villanelles, sonnet sequences, terza rima triplets, and others. The result is poetry that values the past without being confined to it, that seeks to celebrate the kinetic American language without despising the traditions out of which it has developed.

Photograph by Elinor J. George

**Judith Moffett** was born in 1942 and grew up in Cincinnati. She holds a doctorate in American Civilization from the University of Pennsylvania. In 1967/68 she was Fulbright Lecturer in American Studies at the University of Lund, Sweden; she has also taught at several American universities and worked as a Poet-in-the-Schools.

**Louisiana** LSU **State University Press**
Baton Rouge 70803

0-8071-0254-7